Italy

Julie McCulloch

**Heinemann
Library**

Chicago, Illinois

© 2001 Reed Educational & Professional Publishing
Published by Heinemann Library,
an imprint of Reed Educational & Professional Publishing,
Chicago, IL

Customer Service 888-454-2279

Visit our website at www.heinemannlibrary.com

Designed by Tinstar Design
Illustrations by Nicholas Beresford-Davies
Originated by Dot Gradations
Printed by Wing King Tong in Hong Kong.

05 04 03 02 01
10 9 8 7 6 5 4 3 2

Library of Congress Cataloging-in-Publication Data
McCulloch, Julie, 1973-
   Italy / Julie McCulloch.
     p. cm. -- (A world of recipes)
   Includes bibliographical references and index.
   ISBN 1-58810-086-3 (lib. bdg.)   ISBN 1-58810-388-9 (pbk. bdg.)
   1. Cookery, Italian--Juvenile literature. 2. Cookery--Italy--Juvenile literature. [1. Cookery, Italian. 2. Italy--Social life and customs.] I. Title.

TX723 .M395 2001
641.5945--dc21

00-059744

Acknowledgments
The Publishers would like to thank the following for permission to reproduce photographs:
Robert Harding, p.5. All other photographs: Gareth Boden.
Illustration p.45, US Department of Agriculture/US Department of Health and Human Services.

Cover photographs reproduced with permission of Gareth Boden.

Every effort has been made to contact copyright holders of any material reproduced in this book. Any omissions will be rectified in subsequent printings if notice is given to the Publisher.

Some words in this book are in bold, **like this.** You can find out what they mean by looking in the glossary.

Contents

Key

* easy

** medium

*** difficult

Italian Food

SWITZERLAND

AUSTRIA

The Alps

SLOVENIA

Venice

CROATIA

Milan

ITALY

Bologna

BOSNIA-
HERZEGOVINA

FRANCE

Florence

Adriatic Sea

Rome

Naples

SARDINIA

Mediterranean Sea

SICILY

feet HEIGHT meters	
over 13120	over 4000
6560-13120	2000-4000
3277-6557	1000-1999
1640-3277	500-999
656-1637	200-499
under 656	under 200

N
W E
S

| kilometers | 0 | 50 | 100 | 150 | 200 | 250 |
| miles | 0 | | 50 | | 100 | 150 |

Italy is a long, narrow country in southern Europe. Italian cooking is very popular. Some dishes, such as lasagne and ice cream, are made all over the world. Recipes for these dishes are included in this book.

In the past

Cooking in Italy is quite varied. It has been influenced by people from other countries who settled in Italy long ago.

In the eighth century B.C.E., parts of Italy were occupied by the ancient Greeks. The Greeks introduced their foods and ways of cooking, including using flat bread, which may have led to the creation of pizza.

Between the first and fifth centuries C.E., Rome, Italy, was the center of the huge **Roman Empire**. The Romans introduced Italian cooking to their people.

At different times between 1400 and 1700, people from France, Spain, and Germany all ruled parts of Italy. Each brought their own food traditions.

4

Around the country

The climate and soil in Italy are also quite varied. Italians grow all kinds of **grains**, fruits, and vegetables. Italy has a long coastline, so plenty of fresh fish and seafood are used in Italian cooking.

Huge mountains called the Alps separate Italy from Switzerland and France. In the north, wheat, corn, and rice grow on the rich farmland. People use these crops in traditional northern Italian dishes such as *risotto*, made from rice, and *polenta*, a type of flour made from corn, which can be baked or **broiled.**

Many people in Italy like to buy fresh fruit and vegetables from market stalls such as these.

Southern Italy is dry and rocky. Many farmers in this area grow olives both for eating and pressing to make olive oil. Traditional southern Italian dishes include pasta and pizza.

Italian meals

The main meal in Italy usually is eaten in the middle of the day and is made up of three courses. The first course is often a rice or pasta dish. A typical main course contains meat, chicken, or fish. The meal is then rounded off with a dessert.

5

Ingredients

olive oil
mozzarella
Gorgonzola
goat cheese
canned tomatoes
tomatoes
dried pasta
basil
thyme
Parmesan cheese
garlic
arborio rice
rice

Because Italian cooking is so popular, most ingredients are easy to find in stores and supermarkets.

Cheese

Italians use a lot of cheese in their cooking. Four different kinds of Italian cheese are used in this book: Parmesan, mozzarella, Gorgonzola, and goat's cheese. Parmesan is very hard and is usually used finely **grated** or thinly **sliced**. You can buy it ready-grated, but it tastes fresher if you buy a small block and grate it when you need it. Mozzarella is a soft, mild cheese that is used to top pizzas and in other dishes. Gorgonzola is a blue cheese with a strong flavor. There are a lot of different kinds of goat's cheese, too.

Garlic

Garlic is used in many Italian dishes. You can buy fresh garlic cloves in the vegetable section of any grocery store or supermarket.

Herbs

Herbs add flavor to food and often are used in Italian cooking. Three of the most common herbs are basil, oregano, and thyme. Fresh herbs often have more flavor and take less time to cook, but dried herbs can be kept longer. Most of the recipes in this book use dried herbs but suggest how to use fresh ones. A few dishes really need fresh herbs to taste their best!

Oil

Italians use olive oil for **frying** and **drizzling** over pasta, salads, and other dishes. You can use other kinds of oil, such as vegetable or corn oil, but olive oil gives a more genuine Italian flavor, so use it to make these dishes if you can.

Pasta

Pasta is made from flour, water, and sometimes eggs. It is used in many Italian dishes. It comes in many different shapes, each with its own name, such as spaghetti or fusilli. Most supermarkets have a good selection of fresh and dried pasta. Dried pasta takes longer to cook but is less expensive than fresh pasta. It also keeps for a long time.

Rice

Rice is the basis of a famous Italian dish called *risotto*. Risotto is usually made with a special kind of rice called arborio, which gives the risotto the right creamy texture. It can be found in most supermarkets. Often it is just called Italian rice or risotto rice.

Tomatoes

Tomatoes are used in many Italian dishes. In most dishes in this book, you can use either fresh or canned tomatoes.

Before You Begin

Kitchen rules

There are a few basic rules you should always follow when you cook:

- Ask an adult if you can use the kitchen.
- Some cooking processes, especially those involving hot water or oil, can be dangerous. When you see this sign, take extra care or ask an adult to help.
- Wash your hands before you begin.
- Wear an apron to protect your clothes. Tie back long hair.
- Be very careful when using sharp knives.
- Never leave pan handles sticking out—it could be dangerous if you bump into them.
- Always wear oven mitts when lifting things in and out of the oven.
- Wash fruits and vegetables before using them.

How long will it take?

Some of the recipes in this book are quick and easy, and some are more difficult and take longer. The strip across the top of the right-hand page of each recipe tells you how long it will take to cook the dish from start to finish. It also shows how difficult each dish is to make: * (easy), ** (medium), or *** (difficult).

Quantities and measurements

You can see how many people each recipe will serve at the top of the right-hand page, too. Most of the recipes in this book make enough to feed two people. A few of the recipes make enough for four. You can multiply or divide the quantities if you want to cook for more or fewer people.

Ingredients for recipes can be measured in two different ways. Imperial measurements use cups, ounces, and fluid ounces. Metric measurements use grams and milliliters.

In the recipes you will see the following abbreviations:

tbsp = tablespoon   oz = ounce
tsp = teaspoon   lb = pound
ml = milliliters   cm = centimeters
g = gram

Utensils

To cook the recipes in this book, you will need these utensils (as well as kitchen essentials, such as spoons, plates, and bowls):

- baking sheet
- cutting board
- food processor
- frying pan
- grater
- ladle
- large, flat, ovenproof dish
- lemon squeezer

- measuring cup
- rolling pin
- saucepan with lid
- set of measuring spoons
- sharp knife
- colander
- whisk
- toothpicks or skewers

(!) Whenever you use kitchen knives, be very careful.

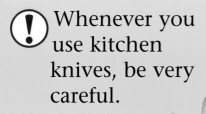

9

Minestrone Soup

Soup often is served as an appetizer in Italy, although it also can be eaten as a light meal with bread. People all over Italy eat Minestrone soup, but the ingredients vary from place to place and from season to season. In winter, more pasta is added to make a thicker, more filling soup. In summer, it might contain seasonal vegetables, such as asparagus and broad beans.

What you need

1/2 onion
1 garlic clove
1 celery stick
1/2 carrot
1/2 cabbage
1 1/2 oz (40 g) dried spaghetti
1 vegetable **bouillon cube**
1 tbsp olive oil
1 cup (200 g) canned chopped tomatoes
1/2 cup (40 g) canned green beans
1 tsp dried or a few sprigs of fresh parsley

What you do

1 **Peel** the onion and garlic clove and finely **chop** them.

2 Thinly **slice** the celery and carrot.

3 Shred the cabbage into small pieces.

4 Break the spaghetti into small pieces, about 3/4 in. (2 cm) long.

5 Put 1 1/4 cups (125 ml) of cold water into a saucepan and bring it to a **boil**. Drop the bouillon cube into the water and stir until it **dissolves**. Put the **stock** aside.

6 Heat the oil in a saucepan over medium heat. Add the chopped onion and garlic, celery, and carrot. **Fry** for 3 minutes.

7 Add the canned tomatoes, vegetable stock, cabbage, canned green beans, and parsley (if you are using dried parsley). Bring to a boil, then **simmer** for 10 minutes.

8 Add the dried spaghetti.

9 Cook the soup for another 8 minutes, stirring from time to time to keep it from sticking to the bottom of the pan. If you are using fresh parsley, add it just before serving the soup.

11

Butternut Squash Soup

Butternut squash has a mild, sweet flavor. If you can't find one, use another kind of squash, such as acorn squash. This smooth butternut squash soup is very filling.

What you need

1 butternut squash
1 onion
1 garlic clove
1 vegetable **bouillon cube**
2 tbsp olive oil
1 1/2 oz (40 g) Parmesan cheese

What you do

1 Using a sharp knife, carefully cut the squash in half lengthwise. You only need half of the squash for this recipe.

2 Scoop the seeds out of the squash with a spoon.

3 Using the same knife, carefully **peel** the squash and **chop** it into small pieces.

4 Peel the onion and garlic clove and finely chop them.

5 Put 2 cups (500 ml) of water into a saucepan and bring it to a **boil**. Drop the bouillon cube into the water and stir until it **dissolves.** Put the **stock** aside.

6 Heat the oil in a saucepan over medium heat. Add the chopped onion, garlic, and squash and **fry** them for 5 minutes.

7 Add the vegetable stock. Bring to a boil, then turn the heat to its lowest setting. **Simmer** the soup for 15 minutes.

8 While the soup is simmering, **grate** the Parmesan cheese.

(!) 9 Pour the soup into a food processor or blender and **blend** until it is smooth.

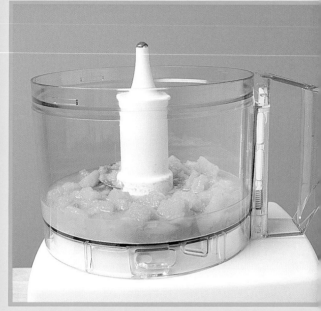

10 Spoon the soup into two bowls and sprinkle grated Parmesan cheese over each.

Polenta and Goat Cheese Salad

Polenta is a type of flour made from ground corn. It is mixed with water, then cooked. Polenta is used in a lot of dishes, especially in the north of Italy. You can serve this dish as an appetizer or light meal. If you cannot find goat cheese, use any type of cheese that is creamy and easy to spread.

What you need

2/3 lb (300 g) polenta
4 oz (100 g) goat cheese
1 tbsp olive oil
1/2 tbsp balsamic or red vinegar
2 cups (50 g) torn lettuce leaves

What you do

1 Slice the polenta about 1/4 in. (about 1/2 cm) thick.

2 Put the polenta slices onto a baking sheet. **Broil** them for about 7 minutes, until they start to turn brown. Turn them over and broil for another 7 minutes.

3 Remove the polenta from the broiler. Spread the goat cheese onto one side of each slice.

4 Put the polenta and cheese back under the broiler for about 5 minutes, until the cheese starts to bubble.

5 Mix the oil and vinegar together. Put the lettuce into a bowl and add the oil and vinegar.

6 Toss the salad with a spoon to coat the leaves with the oil and vinegar.

7 Put the salad onto two plates and arrange the polenta slices on top.

BUYING POLENTA

You can buy polenta in two forms—as flour, or in a form that is ready-to-use. Ready-to-use polenta is baked to form a solid cake. If you can't find this form, buy polenta flour and follow the instructions on the package to make a polenta cake to broil.

Spaghetti Bolognese

In Italy, pasta often is served as an appetizer, rather than as a main course. There are more than 200 different shapes of pasta. Every region has its favorite and its favorite way of serving it. Spaghetti bolognese is named after Bologna, a city in northern Italy.

What you need

1 onion
1 garlic clove
1 tbsp olive oil
3 large mushrooms
1/2 lb (250 g) lean
    ground beef
1 14-oz (400 g) can
    chopped tomatoes
1/2 tsp dried oregano
1/2 tsp dried basil
5 oz (150 g) dried
    spaghetti

What you do

1 **Peel** the onion and garlic clove and finely **chop** them.

2 Thinly **slice** the mushrooms.

(!) 3 Heat the oil in a saucepan over medium heat. Add the chopped onion and garlic and **fry** for 5 minutes.

4 Add the ground beef and cook for another 10 minutes, stirring from time to time, until the meat is brown.

5 Add the canned tomatoes, sliced mushrooms, oregano, and basil. Stir well.

6 Reduce the heat to the lowest setting. **Cover** the pan and cook gently for 20 minutes.

7 Meanwhile, bring a saucepan of water to a **boil**. Carefully add the spaghetti and cook for about 10 minutes, until the spaghetti has just started to get soft.

⚠ 8 **Drain** the spaghetti and put it into two bowls. Spoon the bolognese sauce over the spaghetti.

PASTA SHAPES

Here are some of the most common pasta shapes:

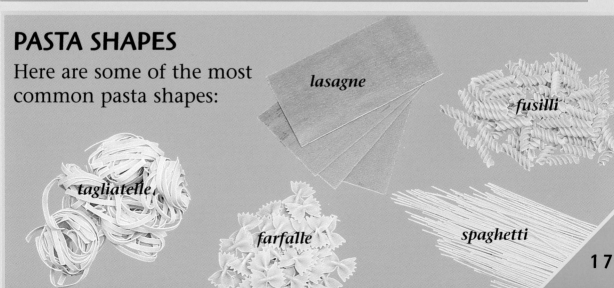

lasagne

fusilli

tagliatelle

farfalle

spaghetti

Pasta Carbonara

Pasta carbonara was first made in Rome. It used to be seen as a poor person's meal, because in the days when meat was expensive, this dish made a small amount of meat go a long way.

What you need

1/4 lb (100 g) smoked bacon
1 garlic clove
2 cups (150 g) pasta shapes (try farfalle, penne, or fusilli)
4 tbsp heavy cream
2 egg yolks
1 1/2 oz (40 g) Parmesan cheese

What you do

1 Using a sharp knife, cut the bacon into small pieces.

2 **Peel** the garlic clove and finely **chop** it.

3 To separate the egg yolks from the whites, gently crack open one of the eggs over a small bowl. Keeping the yolk in one half of the shell, let the white drip out into the bowl. Pass the yolk between the two halves of the shell until all the white has dripped out. Drop the yolk into a separate bowl. Repeat this with the second egg.

4 **Grate** the Parmesan cheese.

5 Bring a saucepan of water to a **boil**. Add the pasta shapes, turn down the heat, and **simmer** for about 10 minutes, until the pasta has just started to get soft.

(!) 6 While the pasta is cooking, gently **fry** the bacon for 3 minutes.

7 Add the chopped garlic and fry for 1 minute.

8 Add the cream to the egg yolks and **beat** them with a fork. Add the cream and egg mixture to the bacon in the frying pan and heat gently for 2 minutes, stirring all the time to make sure the egg cooks.

(!) 9 Drain the pasta by emptying it into a colander. Put it into two bowls and spoon on the sauce. Sprinkle with Parmesan cheese.

Lasagne

Lasagne is a pasta dish first made in northern Italy. It is **baked** in the oven. Double the recipe for the bolognese sauce shown on page 16.

What you need

4 servings bolognese sauce

1/4 cup (100 g) Parmesan cheese

2 tbsp butter or margarine

13 strips lasagne pasta

1/4 cup (30 g) **cornstarch**

2 1/2 cups (600 ml) milk

What you do

1 Follow steps 1 through 6 of the recipe on page 16, making twice the amount of bolognese sauce shown there.

2 **Grate** the Parmesan cheese.

3 **Preheat** the oven to 350°F (180°C).

4 Melt the butter or margarine in a saucepan over low heat. Take the saucepan off the heat and gradually add the cornstarch, stirring all the time, to make a thick paste.

5 Keeping the pan off the heat, gradually stir the milk into the paste.

6 Put the sauce back on the heat. Stir it until it becomes thick and starts to bubble.

7 Coat the bottom of a 9 x 13 in. (22.5 x 32.5 cm.) ovenproof dish with cooking spray. Spread one third of the bolognese sauce across the bottom. Cover the sauce with a layer of lasagne pasta, then spread one third of the white sauce over the pasta.

8 Repeat this process twice more, making sure the final layer of white sauce completely covers the pasta.

9 Sprinkle the grated Parmesan cheese over the top.

10 **Cover** the lasagne with foil and bake it for 20 minutes.

11 Remove the foil and bake for another 15 minutes, until the top of the lasagne is brown and bubbling.

12 Cut the lasagne into four servings.

Cheese and Tomato Pizza

Pizzas were first made in Naples, a city in southern Italy. This recipe tells you how to make a basic cheese and tomato pizza. You can use it as a base and add different toppings, such as salami, ham, sliced mushrooms, or sliced red peppers.

What you need

For the pizza crust:
1 cup (125 g)
   self-rising flour
1/2 tsp salt
2 tbsp olive oil
1/3 cup (75 ml) warm
   water

For the topping:
1 onion
1 tbsp olive oil
1 cup (200 g) canned
   chopped tomatoes
1/2 tsp dried oregano
1/2 tsp dried basil
1/4 cup (125 g)
   mozzarella cheese

What you do

1 **Preheat** the oven to 450°F (230°C).

2 Put the flour and salt in a large bowl. Add the olive oil, stirring all the time.

3 Slowly pour the warm water into the flour and oil mixture, stirring while you pour. When the water is mixed into the flour, use your hands to form the mixture into a ball.

4 Sprinkle some flour onto a cutting board. Turn the ball of pizza dough out onto the cutting board, then **knead** it until it is smooth and soft.

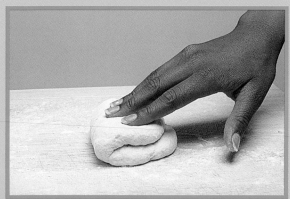

5 Using a rolling pin, roll out the dough into a circle about 12 in. (30 cm) wide. Put the pizza crust onto a baking sheet and set it aside.

6 **Peel** the onion and finely **chop** it.

⚠ 7 Heat the oil in a saucepan over medium heat. Add the onion and **fry** for 3 minutes.

8 Add the tomatoes, oregano, and basil to the saucepan. **Simmer** this tomato sauce for about 15 minutes.

9 Spoon the tomato sauce over the pizza curst, spreading it with the back of a spoon.

10 Thinly **slice** the mozzarella cheese and arrange the slices over the top of the pizza.

11 Put the pizza into the oven and **bake** for 10 minutes.

Potato and Blue Cheese Calzone

Calzones are pizzas that are folded over to make a half circle. Because the filling is sealed inside the crust, calzones are ideal for picnics. Before you begin, you need to make a pizza crust by following steps 2 through 5 of the pizza recipe on page 22.

What you need

1 pizza crust
1 onion
1 medium potato
2 tbsp olive oil
1/4 cup (75 g) blue cheese, such as Gorgonzola
1/4 cup (75 g) mozzarella cheese

What you do

1 Make a pizza crust by following steps 2 through 5 of the recipe on page 22.

2 **Preheat** the oven to 450°F (230°C).

3 **Peel** the onion and finely **chop** it.

4 Peel or scrub the potato and chop it into small pieces.

5 Heat the oil in a frying pan over medium heat. Add the chopped onion and **fry** for 3 minutes.

6 Bring a saucepan of water to a **boil.** Add the potato pieces and boil them for about 5 minutes, until they are soft. **Drain** the water from the potatoes by emptying the pan into a colander.

7 Cut the blue cheese and mozzarella cheese into small pieces.

8 Add the cheeses and fried onions to the potatoes and mix together.

9 Put the pizza crust onto a baking sheet. Spoon the cheese and potato mixture onto half of the crust.

10 Fold the pizza crust in half so all the filling is covered. Using your fingers, pinch the edges of the crust together to seal the filling inside.

11 Put the calzone into the oven and **bake** for 15 minutes.

Shrimp and Mushroom Risotto

What you need

1 onion

3 large mushrooms

1 oz (25 g) Parmesan cheese

1 vegetable **bouillon cube**

1 tbsp olive oil

1 1/4 cup (200 g) arborio rice

a few fresh oregano leaves or 1/2 tsp dried oregano

a few fresh basil leaves or 1/2 tsp dried basil

1/4 lb (100 g) cooked shrimp

Risotto is a traditional Italian rice dish. It is a very filling main course.

What you do

1 **Peel** the onion and finely **chop** it.

2 **Slice** the mushrooms.

3 **Grate** the Parmesan cheese.

4 Put 1 1/3 cups (225 ml) of water into a saucepan and bring it to a **boil**. Drop the bouillon cube into the water and stir until it **dissolves**. Put the **stock** aside.

5 Heat the oil in a large pan over medium heat. Add the chopped onion and **fry** for about 3 minutes, until the onion is soft.

6 Add the rice to the pan. Cook for another 5 minutes, stirring all the time to make sure the rice does not stick.

7 Put 3 tbsp of the vegetable stock in a ladle and add to the pan. Stir well.

8 Add the sliced mushrooms. If you are using dried herbs, add them now.

9 When the stock has been soaked up, add another 2 tbsp of stock. Keep stirring the risotto and adding more stock until the rice is soft. This should take about 20 minutes.

10 Stir in the shrimp and cook for 3 minutes.

11 Turn off the heat, then stir in the grated Parmesan cheese.

12 If you are using fresh herbs, chop the basil leaves and stir them in. Spoon the risotto onto two plates and sprinkle the oregano leaves on top.

Baked Fish and Potatoes

Many Italian people buy fish and seafood that is still alive. This ensures that it is as fresh as possible when it is time to cook it. In this dish, you can use fresh or frozen fish. If you use frozen fish, make sure you **defrost** it before you want to use it.

What you need

1 medium potato
1 tsp dried thyme
2 fish fillets
1 tbsp olive oil

What you do

1 **Preheat** the oven to 425°F (220°C).

2 **Peel** or scrub the potato and thinly **slice** it. Put the slices into a saucepan and add just enough water to cover them.

3 **Boil** the potato slices in the water for 5 minutes, until they are just starting to get soft. **Drain** the water from the potatoes by emptying the pan into a colander.

4 Spray an ovenproof dish with cooking spray.

5 Arrange the potato slices in the bottom of the dish. Sprinkle the thyme over the potatoes.

6 Place the fish fillets on top of the potatoes.

7 **Drizzle** the oil over the fish fillets.

8 Put the dish in the oven and **bake** for 20 minutes.

ADDED OLIVES

Try adding olives to this dish, if you like them.
Put 1 tbsp of black olives with the pits removed
onto the potatoes at the same time as you add the fish.

Eggplant and Mozzarella Towers

This **vegetarian** main course is served with *pesto,* a sauce made from fresh basil, Parmesan cheese, and pine nuts. The recipe for pesto appears on page 36. You can also buy it already made.

What you need

1 small eggplant
1 large tomato
1/4 lb (125 g) mozzarella cheese
2 tbsp pesto (see page 36)
a little olive oil

What you do

1 **Preheat** the oven to 375°F (190°C).

2 Cut off the top and bottom of the eggplant and throw them away. Slice the rest into four slices.

3 Put the eggplant slices onto a baking sheet. **Broil** them for about 10 minutes, then turn them over and broil them on the other side for another 10 minutes.

4 Meanwhile, slice the tomato and mozzarella cheese into four slices.

5 Rub a small amount of oil onto a baking sheet with a paper towel.

6 Build the towers like this:
- Put 2 eggplant slices onto the baking sheet.
- Put a tomato slice on top of each eggplant slice.
- Put a mozzarella slice on top of each tomato slice.
- Add another layer of eggplant, tomato, and mozzarella slices.

7 Stick a toothpick or skewer through each tower to hold it together.

8 Put the towers in the oven and **bake** for 10 minutes.

9 Take the towers out of the oven and put them onto plates. Carefully take out the toothpicks or skewers.

10 Spoon the pesto over the top of the towers.

Vegetable Frittata

Frittata is the Italian version of an omelette. It can be made with all kinds of vegetables. You need to use a frying pan with an ovenproof handle for this recipe, because you need to put the pan into the oven.

What you need

1 onion
1 garlic clove
1 red pepper
1 zucchini
3 eggs
1 oz (25 g) Parmesan cheese
1 medium potato
1 tbsp olive oil
1 tsp dried thyme

What you do

1 **Preheat** the oven to (400°F) 200°C.

2 **Peel** the onion and garlic clove and finely **chop** them.

3 Cut the red pepper in half. Scoop out the seeds, then chop the flesh into small pieces.

4 Thinly **slice** the zucchini.

5 Crack the eggs into a small bowl. **Beat** them with a fork or whisk until the yolk and white are mixed.

6 **Grate** the Parmesan cheese.

7 Peel or scrub the potato. Cut it into small pieces about 1/2 in. (1 cm) thick. Put the pieces of potato into a saucepan and cover them with water.

8 **Boil** the potato pieces for 5 minutes, until they are just starting to get soft. **Drain** them by emptying the pan into a colander.

9 Heat the oil in an ovenproof frying pan over medium heat.

⚠ **10** Add the chopped onion, garlic, and red pepper, sliced zucchini, cooked potato pieces, and thyme to the frying pan. **Fry** for 5 minutes.

11 Pour the beaten eggs into the pan, covering all the vegetables. Cook for 3 minutes.

12 Take the pan off the heat and sprinkle the grated Parmesan cheese over the mixture.

13 Put the pan into the oven and cook the frittata for 15 minutes, until the egg is **set** and golden brown.

14 Take the pan out, run a knife around the edge, and slide the frittata onto a plate. Serve it in slices.

Bruschetta

Bruschetta is the name for Italian garlic bread. It is made with crusty Italian bread, which can be found in most supermarkets. Fresh parsley tastes and looks best sprinkled on top, but if you cannot find any, use dried parsley instead. Bruschetta makes a good snack and is also delicious served with soup.

What you need

crusty Italian bread
1 garlic clove
1 handful of fresh
  parsley leaves
2 tbsp olive oil
salt

What you do

1 **Slice** the bread into four 1/2-in. (1-cm) pieces.

2 **Peel** the garlic clove but do not **chop** it.

3 Finely chop the fresh parsley leaves.

4 Put the slices of bread onto a baking sheet and **broil** for about 3 minutes. Turn them over and broil for another 3 minutes. The toasted bread should be golden brown.

5 Rub the garlic clove over one side of each slice of bread. The bread acts like a **grater** so that the garlic is cut into tiny pieces and spread over the bread.

6 Sprinkle the bread with the salt and chopped parsley.

7 Carefully **drizzle** the olive oil over the top. Eat your bruschetta immediately, before it gets soggy!

OTHER BREAD

If you can't find crusty Italian bread, try making bruschetta with other types of crusty bread, such as slices of a long French stick or baguette.

Pesto

Pesto is a sauce made from fresh basil, Parmesan cheese, and pine nuts. In Italy, pesto is eaten with all kinds of dishes. It is stirred into soups, added to pasta, or spooned over vegetables.

You can buy pesto already made, but it is easy to make your own. It will keep in the refrigerator for up to two weeks in a clean jar with a lid.

What you need

1 garlic clove
1 oz fresh basil leaves
2 tbsp pine nuts
4 tbsp olive oil
1 oz (30 g) Parmesan cheese

What you do

1 **Peel** the garlic clove.

2 Put the basil, peeled garlic clove, pine nuts, and olive oil in a food processor or a blender. Make sure the lid is on properly.

3 Turn the food processor or blender on to its highest speed. **Blend** the ingredients together to make a thick, creamy sauce.

4 Pour the sauce into a bowl.

5 **Grate** the Parmesan cheese into the sauce and stir everything together well.

PURPLE PESTO

There are different flavors and colors of basil. Try using purple basil to make your pesto. You will get a beautiful bright-purple sauce to stir into pasta!

Chocolate Risotto

In Italy, risotto is not always a **savory** dish. Here's a recipe for a chocolate one! It tastes like a delicious chocolate rice pudding. Arborio rice—sometimes called Italian rice or risotto rice—works best.

What you need

1 1/2 oz (40 g) semisweet chocolate
1 1/3 cups (300 ml) milk
1 tbsp sugar
2 tbsp butter or margarine
1/2 cup (80 g) rice
1/4 cup (25 g) raisins

What you do

1 **Grate** the chocolate. This is easiest when the chocolate is very cold.

2 Put the milk and sugar into a saucepan. Heat it over low heat until it is hot but not **boiling.**

3 Melt the butter or margarine in another saucepan. Add the rice and stir well so that the rice is coated with the butter or margarine.

4 Add 2 tbsp of the hot milk to the rice and stir it in.

5 When the rice has soaked up the milk, add another 2 tbsp milk. Keep stirring the risotto and adding more milk until the rice is soft. This should take about 20 minutes.

6 Stir all the raisins and almost all the grated chocolate into the risotto.

7 Divide the risotto into two bowls and sprinkle each with the leftover chocolate.

SWEET RISOTTOS

Try experimenting with other sweet risottos.
Instead of grated chocolate, try adding honey, jam,
or chopped dried apricots.

Vanilla Ice Cream

Italy is famous for its ice cream. It is easy to make your own, but you need to stir it regularly while it freezes to keep lumps of ice from forming.

What you need

1 ¹/₃ cup (300 ml) milk
1 tsp vanilla extract
4 egg yolks
1 cup (100 g) powdered sugar
1 ¹/₃ cups (300 ml) heavy cream

What you do

1 Put the milk and vanilla extract into a saucepan. Heat over low heat until the mixture is hot but not **boiling**.

2 To separate the egg yolks from the whites, crack open one of the eggs over a bowl. Keeping the yolk in one half of the shell, let the white drip out into the bowl. Pass the yolk between the two halves of the shell until all the white has dripped out. Put the yolk into a separate bowl. Repeat this with the other three eggs.

3 Add the sugar to the bowl of egg yolks. **Beat** the egg yolks and sugar together until they are well mixed.

4 Gradually add the hot milk into the egg and sugar mixture, stirring all the time.

5 Carefully pour the mixture back into the saucepan. Cook it over low heat until it thickens, stirring all the time.

6 Pour the mixture into a bowl, then stir in the cream.

7 Put the mixture into the freezer. After 1 hour, take the bowl out and **mash** the mixture with a fork to break up any lumps.

8 Mash the ice cream every hour until it is **set**. This should take about 4 to 5 hours, depending on how cold your freezer is.

OTHER FLAVORS

In Italy, there are countless flavors of ice cream.
Make up your own flavors by adding extra ingredients, such as chocolate chips or mashed strawberries to the mixture at the same time you add the cream.

Lemon Granita

Granita is a frozen fruit pudding. It has tiny granules of ice in it, which is how it got its name. In Italy, it often is topped with whipped cream and served with a sweet pastry. Granita is easy to make and very refreshing.

What you need

2 lemons
4 tbsp sugar

What you do

(!) **1** Put the sugar into a saucepan with 1 1/3 (300 ml) cups of water. Bring the mixture to a **boil**, stirring until all the sugar **dissolves**. Boil for 5 minutes.

2 Allow the sugar and water mixture to **cool**.

3 Using a lemon squeezer, squeeze the juice out of the lemons into a bowl.

4 Add the cooled sugar and water mixture to the lemon juice. Stir well.

5 Put the bowl into the freezer. After an hour, take the bowl out of the freezer and **mash** the mixture with a fork to break up any big lumps.

6 Put the bowl back into the freezer. After another hour, take it out of the freezer and mash it again with a fork before you serve it.

VARIATIONS

You can make granita with other types of fruit. Try replacing the lemon juice with orange or grapefruit juice or with mashed strawberries.

More Books

Cookbooks

Bisignano, Alphonse, and Jeanetter Swofford. *Cooking the Italian Way.* Minneapolis, Minn.: Lerner Publications, 1982.

Buicchi, Edwina. *Italian Food and Drink.* Danbury, Conn.: Franklin Watts, Inc., 1987.

Ridgewell, Jenny. *A Taste of Italy.* Florence, Ky.: Thomson Learning, 1993.

Books About Italy

Boast, Clare. *Next Stop, Italy.* Chicago, Ill.: Heinemann Library, 1998.

Hausam, Josephine Sander. *Italy.* Milwaukee, Wis.: Gareth Stevens, 1999.

Comparing Weights and Measures

3 teaspoons = 1 tablespoon	1 tablespoon = 1/2 fluid ounce	1 teaspoon = 5 milliliters
4 tablespoons = 1/4 cup	1 cup = 8 fluid ounces	1 tablespoon = 15 milliliters
5 1/3 tablespoons = 1/3 cup	1 cup = 1/2 pint	1 cup = 240 milliliters
8 tablespoons = 1/2 cup	2 cups = 1 pint	1 quart = 1 liter
10 2/3 tablespoons = 2/3 cup	4 cups = 1 quart	1 ounce = 28 grams
12 tablespoons = 3/4 cup	2 pints = 1 quart	1 pound = 454 grams
16 tablespoons = 1 cup	4 quarts = 1 gallon	

Healthy Eating

This diagram shows which foods you should eat to stay healthy. You should eat 6–11 servings a day of foods from the bottom of the pyramid. Eat 2–4 servings of fruits and 3–5 servings of vegetables a day. You should also eat 2–3 servings from the milk group and 2–3 servings from the meat group. Eat only a few of the foods from the top of the pyramid.

Italian cooking is very healthy. It includes a lot of pasta and some rice, along with bread and pizza crust. Italian people also eat a lot of fresh vegetables, as well as some meat and fish. Many of their desserts are made with fruit.

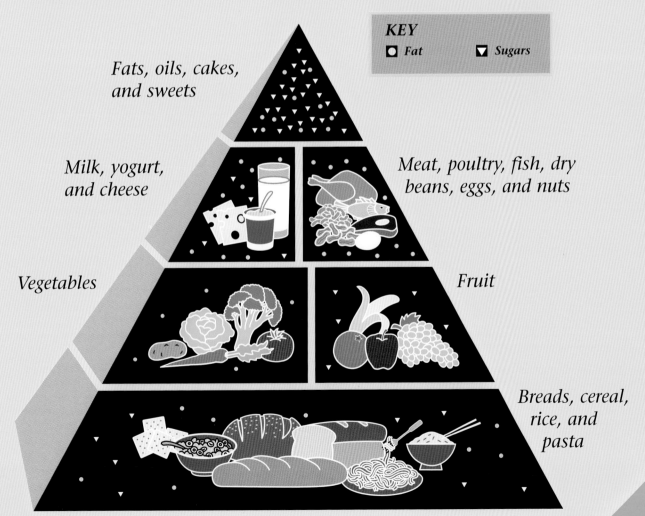

KEY
◻ *Fat*   ◺ *Sugars*

Fats, oils, cakes, and sweets

Milk, yogurt, and cheese

Meat, poultry, fish, dry beans, eggs, and nuts

Vegetables

Fruit

Breads, cereal, rice, and pasta

Glossary

bake to cook something in the oven

beat to mix something together strongly, for example egg yolks and whites

blend to mix ingredients together in a blender or food processor

boil to cook a liquid on the stovetop until it bubbles and steams strongly

bouillon cube small cube of powdered vegetable or meat flavoring used to make a base for soups or sauces

chop to cut something into pieces using a knife

cool to allow hot food to become cold, especially before putting it in the refrigerator

cornstarch powder made from corn that is used to thicken sauces and puddings

cover to put a lid on a pan or foil over a dish

defrost to allow something that is frozen to come to room temperature

dissolve to stir something, for example sugar, until it disappears into a liquid

drain to remove liquid from a pan or can

drizzle to pour something slowly onto a surface in a very thin stream

fry to cook something by placing it in hot oil or fat

grain seed of cereal plants, such as wheat, corn, or rice

grate to shred something by rubbing it back and forth over a utensil that has a rough surface

knead to mix ingredients into a smooth dough

mash to crush something until it is soft and pulpy

peel to remove the skin of a fruit or vegetable

preheat to turn on the oven in advance, so that it is hot when you are ready to use it

Roman Empire period in history from around 100 B.C.E. to 400 C.E., during which the government of Rome controlled much of what is now Europe

savory dish that is not sweet

set to become firm after chilling or baking

simmer to cook a liquid on the stovetop just under a boil

slice to cut something into thin, flat pieces

stock broth made by slowly cooking meat or vegetables in water or by dissolving a cube of powdered meat flavoring in water

thaw to allow something that has been frozen to come to room temperature

toss to mix ingredients together roughly, as in a salad

vegetarian diet that usually does not include meat or fish, and that sometimes does not include eggs or dairy products; person who follows such a diet

Index